Coming Home

the journey back to myself

Catherine Quiring, MA, LMHC

for Maggie and Jenna,

for holding space and celebrating my writing

I am home

I am home
I can't say I wandered far away

More like
Parts of me were missing

They got
Stuffed down
Shoved in a closet
Stuck in the basement
Swallowed
Ignored
Locked outside

But now
They've been welcomed home
And I am all of me
And I am here*

---

* *I AM: Poems for Expansion and Renewal*

Contents

x

Author's Note:

Dear Reader,

I hope my words and experiences resonate with you and aid you on your journey home to yourself.

In my writing, I often speak of parts of me. I learned this through my favorite therapeutic modality, Internal Family Systems, also known as IFS.

Relating to myself like a family of parts inside, rather than reactions that need to be controlled, has been a fundamental and revolutionary part of my healing journey. It is why I feel at home inside, why my inner world is so full of life, and why I feel connected to spirit/source/self all the time.

As you read about things that were hard for me, I want to give space for any reactions you are having. What I'm writing may feel like an extreme response to what felt much more benign to you, such as your religious experiences. That's okay. I understand that I am often way more intense than neurotypical people, and I experience things intensely. And I love that about me. I hope my intensity lights you up and inspires you.

Be bold, be brave, be you,

Catherine

Introduction

Self-trust is what set me free to be me. Not what someone else told me I should be. Not what I felt pressured to be. Just me. The glorious humanness of my full self.

Trusting myself again led me back to my own knowing. It gave me back to myself. I was able to move back into my life. I am now able to live an embodied life.

Self-compassion was also a key player in this journey home. Home to what I think and want. Home to my desires. Home to my feelings. Home to my body. And also home to my soul. I have a relationship with myself and live inside myself again. And it is so sweet being home.

Authoritarian Christianity is one of the forces that led me away from myself—the subtle but insistent demand to be a good Christian, to hollow myself out to let the holy spirit fill me. The message to follow God and mistrust myself was in the air, the words, and the communion grape-juice of my upbringing.

Another force that led me away from myself is ableist meritocracy, a system where "success, value, and opportunities are determined by abilities that favor able-bodied and neurotypical individuals, while marginalizing or devaluing those with disabilities".

As I released myself from authoritarian Christianity and ableist meritocracy and reconnected with myself, I discovered *neurodivergence*. For me, neurodivergence is the rich inner world that I have reclaimed and made a wonderful place in which to reside again. Knowing myself, understanding myself, and being in relationship with myself from a place of curiosity and compassion— this is where life is and from where I can expand to be all that I am.

Self-trust is not *blind* trust. I'm not expecting myself to be perfect. I don't trust myself to be perfect. I'm not. But now I know that I am human and that I am good inside. I know that any internal struggles I have come from parts of me that feel alone and desperately want to help or protect me. I can trust that they want what's best for me. I am free to listen to them with curiosity and compassion. To build a bridge. To let them know they're not alone anymore. To have a relationship of attunement and presence. To heal.

This might seem like strange language to you. Talking about parts of myself as if they were sentient beings. But this is our truest human experience. Think "Inside Out". Emotions as little people trying desperately to help us navigate this world. We are not robots. We are not sinners with emotions to tame and desires to control. Our emotions, desires, impulses, and actions are more than they appear. They are us. They are clues to what's happening. They are our way through. They are not nuisances. We *need* them. Without them, we get stuck. We can't grow or move forward. It's like parts of us calcify or are stuck on repeat until our emotions and body sensations can help us through. Our thoughts are important too, but they usually come last. Our body knows first what's happening and what we need. And we need our nervous systems, body movements, emotions, thoughts, beliefs, and images to all help us as a team to move through.

I love indigenous wisdom and way of seeing the world. Everything is alive. Everything is kin. And just about everything can be medicine. The ways we move through our experiences are like medicine for us. One of my special interests lately has been identifying these medicines and signs that our bodies feel safe and have moved through. Some I've found include: grief, crying, body shaking, burping, music, nature, vibrations, rhythms, cycles of life, compassion, curiosity, play, awe, and wonder. A lot of the things that polite society has told us we shouldn't do and a capitalist society has said is a distraction from productivity. Be reasonable. Be strong. Be nice. Be polite and regal. Be productive. Be successful. Don't think, don't feel, don't know. Fit in. Go with the flow. Be an image that brings you success. Be a productive machine that brings you success.

But success doesn't satisfy. It is a hollow reward. And we have become hollow inside to pursue it.

Our bodies don't lie. When you know and express what is true and deep, it resonates. It vibrates. It gives you goosebumps. It warms your heart. It makes you feel alive. It makes you weep with knowing and relief.

I want you to experience this too. And I hope my story becomes wings that take you there.

Growing Up

I am free

I am full and free,
proud to be me.
I live and lap life up.

My neighbor friend,
she and I spin
and whirl around her room.

We play "Footloose"
and dance,
delightfully kicking off shoes.

I am fully myself,
I am nothing else.
I feel free, and whole,
and mine.

I am not alone.
I have always known
I am connected
to myself and the divine.

Spun from pure glory
I know my story.
And I hold it dear
to my heart.

I cherish my life
A free spirit, I am,
Following every adventure,

Curiosity calls, and I answer
Skipping along to its beat.

A Funny Feeling

have patience,
for God is patient too…
warbles from my Fisher Price record player.

I can play it slow, or fast, or regular.
When you play it slow, it's deep and low.
I like playing around with the settings.
I think it's funny.

But…I also have a funny feeling in my tummy
when I listen to this song.
Which apparently I do a lot because my adult self still
remembers all the words.

I don't know why exactly,
but it doesn't sit right.

Question weaving

My first memories of
our Southern Baptist Church
are woven of
Sunday School,
blood-red pews,
and Bible stories.

God saved Noah,
and lots of animals,
but killed lots of other people
with lots of water.

I learn this story in Sunday School
as I eat my snack.
The tickle of orange rind
spraying my nose,
its fresh scent filling the air,
as I listen.

I must be less than 5.
I am wearing a black trash bag
turned into a shirt of sorts,
and I don't like it.
I think it's supposed to keep us clean.
I tell my parents later,
and they don't like it either.

But they do like God.
They must not care that he killed all those people.

I stand in the blood-red pew
singing another blood-hymn
about how Jesus washes us clean
with his blood.
I must be less than 6.

How does this make any sense to anyone?
And why are we talking about blood all the time?
Blood is gross, not clean.
I don't want to wash in anyone's blood.

I don't like it.
I think my parents do.
The other people around me seem to like it too.

I sit in a white concrete building
looking at pictures of white Jesus
surrounded by white bodies like mine.
I must be less than 7.

The Sunday School teacher reads us a Bible verse.
I'll summarize it for you:
We are bad, but God will make us good.

I don't understand why we're bad.
Didn't God "make us in his image?"
Aren't we "precious in his sight?"

I don't like it.
But the teacher tells us this is
"good news."
These are the last times I remember feeling uncertain

about God and his choices. Before I was 7.

After that, I know:
God is always right,
God is always good.
And I am good for knowing this
and defending God.

The Prayer

It was supposed to be the happiest day of my life. The day I "asked Jesus into my heart." The best day. A day my parents longed for, and one they celebrated for years. I got a necklace to commemorate the experience—a 14-carat gold key with a heart carved into it. I wore it around my neck.

It was also the day I stepped out of my life.

I was 7.

I was sitting in a pew like every other Sunday, but on this Sunday there was a guest evangelist who was known for sharing the gospel with children. He shared it to me all right. At some point in the sermon, he said, *"You are sinful and wicked. God cannot be around sin. You can't get to God on your own. You need to ask Jesus into your heart!"*

I found myself in shock. Disoriented. Wait—you're saying my love for God is not enough? I have been loving God my whole life. Why is that not enough? Once the shock wore off, I clambered up to the front to pray with the preacher:

"Jesus…" he said.
"Jesus…" I repeated.
"I am a sinner."
"I am a sinner."
"I need you to save me."

"I need you to save me."
"Please forgive me of my sins, and come into my heart."
"Please forgive me of my sins, and come into my heart."

I was whisked off by happy parents and others congratulating me and welcoming me into the family of God. That part felt good…kind of…mostly.

This was the last day for a long, long time, that I lived inside myself. I was aware of this, even from this young age. I came to call this *side-stepping myself*.

I exchanged an embodied life for a soul "sold-out" to Christ. I learned to watch myself and manage myself so I wouldn't hurt anyone unintentionally or sin by accident.

I tried to hollow myself out so the Holy Spirit could fill me. I was told I was supposed to be an empty vessel for the lord. And I was supposed to be pure. And I tried so hard. I tried through elementary school, I tried through middle school, I tried through high school, I tried through college.

In the process, I stuffed, avoided, swallowed, and attempted to cut off all the feelings and parts of me that were not acceptable. *Empty & pure. Acceptable to God. Right with God. No self—only God.*

I Have To

My sister wants to use my hair bow. I don't really want to share. But I'm supposed to.

I'm supposed to be nice and good and generous no matter what anyone else does to me. They tell me that's what God wants. God wants me to be nice and good and generous.

And I have to if I'm going to be a good Christian. I don't always want to be nice. I don't understand why I can't just be me. But they tell me it's life or death.

If I want to go to heaven and be with God I have to be nice and good and generous. So, I'll make myself do that. And squash out the parts of me that want anything else. That's the only way to be safe. The only way to be good. The only way.

So, I tell my sister she can borrow my hair bow, as my gut twists inside. I have a tight smile on my face, but I do it.

The next day, I ask if I can borrow her hair bow, and she refuses. I'm not allowed to think, *not fair!* I have to be sacrificially generous, so I swallow it, and say okay, and keep going the best I can. I can't show that it bothers me, or I risk being selfish. I have to hide it. Have to hide any part of me that's not willingly, gladly generous.

The Birthday Party

It's my second-grade birthday party.
There's a rainbow sign out front
and my friends inside.
My home-sewn azure
princess dress
is a little itchy, but I feel special.

It's time to open presents.

It's a Scrabble game.
I already have that.

It comes out of my mouth
                              before I can think.
…I don't know yet that it's going to cause
                                         a revolution,
                                              a ripple effect
that will touch every crevice of my world.

It is the last moment,
the very last moment
I am myself,
the last time I am at home
  in
    my
      body.

Because it is then I realize—
                              I am dangerous.

I thought I fixed it with The Prayer.
I thought I had it covered because I never intentionally
hurt anyone.
I didn't know I could unintentionally hurt them.

This is bad.
This is very bad.

I am bad.
I am sinful.
                  ...unless
I can watch myself enough,
be alert enough
to prevent
                  it.

I pack myself away

I pack myself away
Set myself up with a small bag
and scurry her off
into somewhere no one can find her
Not even my conscious mind.

She goes away
—deep into my body.
And stows away as quietly as she can.
She pauses her life
for me,
for our survival.

The disconnection is our safety.
I cannot not know she is there or I could be found out
by the ever-seeing God who searches the deepest
recesses of a man's heart to see if he is true to him.
A man's world. A man's rules. A man's all-knowing
God.

Terrorizing a little girl;
making escape from the all-seeing eye of Mordor
the only option.

The exchange

I exchange my embodied life
for a life "sold-out" to Christ.

In the process,
I stuff,
avoid,
swallow,
and try to cut off
all the feelings and
          parts of me that are
                    not acceptable.

                              Prune
                                        myself.

Surrender to God.
Cling to God.
Abide in God.
Empty & pure.
Acceptable to God.
Right with God.
No self—only God.

16

I don't trust myself

There is turning in on myself
I feel small
like I'm moving into the
 fetal
position.
So small.
So invisible.

Confusion in my brain and body.
I must not know.
Because they disagree.

I can't disagree.
I would be in rebellion.
They know more than me.
They have more experience than me.
I'm supposed to trust them.

My mind whirs,
trying to find a place
to land,
to understand.

A refuge.
But I cannot.
I cannot exist.

So, I will rationalize
and circularize
until my thoughts spin me

in a never-ending circle.
Until I throw them into a garbage pile inside.
And tell them to go away.

My gut drops.
Then flip-flops.
It drops again.

My sacral chakra is in pain
shrinking in on itself.

My root chakra tight and closed.

My legs rigid
and tense.
Muscles tight.

My traps are tight as well,
up into my neck.
My shoulders turned in toward my heart.
Protect.
Get smaller.
Shrink.
Don't trust.
You're wrong.
You have to trust them.

I try so hard

I try so hard.
To be a good Christian.
To empty myself out for God.
To be a good witness.
To be pure.
To be holy.
To be what God wants me to be.

I try so hard.
I try through elementary school.
I try through middle school.
I try through high school.
I try through college.

I try so so so so so so hard.
I try so fucking hard.

Emotion Eater

I gulp in the emotions
Swallow them down so fast
I can't tell
the flavor
of them.

Don't let them see.
Don't let anyone know
the emotions were
          here.

Emotions,
I am taught,
are dangerous.
They are not
to be trusted.
Like my deceitful
heart—
they will always lead me
astray...
away,
          from God.

Don't they know
I can't live without emotions?
I eat and drink and breathe them.
They are my closest kin.

It is not safe for me to see
the feelings.

I stuff them down,
hoping they will go away.
My body feels how tenuous it is,
how impossible it is
to carry on this way
and yet, what choice do I have?

My body suffers.
It holds too much pain.
Too much
unresolved grief,
and angst,
and bitter disappointment.

Purity

Purity drains me of my life.
A siphon of all that is delicious, and sensual, and dark,
and deep.

A digging out, an excavation, of the earth of my life. The
rich soil dumped out in the dump where it cannot nurture
me or any other life.

A hollowing out of all imagination, replaced with the
concrete of linear thought,
the dogmas that are taught,
the rational and right way to think
and to be.

The dark internal caverns full of mystery and magic
Are roped off, barricaded, and neglected.
They exist for me only in
passing wisps of memory—
even then,
they are relegated and retaught:
must be a dangerous myth,
don't even think it,
let alone go there.

Once Purity empties me,
it transforms into
a ruler to judge me by,
which must be examined and marked at every moment—
an introspective micro-managing,
I ask myself every moment:

Am I Christian enough?
Sold-out enough?
Am I...
Pure of heart?
Pure of thought?

Do I have pure motives?
Am I doing everything for God?
Doing what Jesus would do?
Honoring my parents?
Taking captive every thought?
Keeping my temple pure?
Eradicating my sexuality?
Warding off every temptation?

If the answer is yes, I pass—
and I have...
the relief of a moment
the reward of a gold star,
the title of the golden child,
and the assurance of my identity as a sheep♦ entering the
Kingdom of Heaven.
If the answer is no, I fail—
and I find instead...
guilt and shame, conviction and repentance, fear of
backsliding and falling away if it continues (will I miss
the Rapture?), fear of God's displeasure, fear of myself,
inner judgment for not having enough discipline, fear

♦ "and he will separate the people one from another as a shepherd
separates the sheep from the goats. He will put the sheep on his right
and the goats on his left." (Matthew 25:32b)

that I might be identified as a goat♦ and sent away from
the Kingdom.

After years of this,
I am left a wisp of a person,
No substance to draw from.
Only the shell of a rigid statue left,
Hollow inside.*

♦ "and he will separate the people one from another as a shepherd
separates the sheep from the goats. He will put the sheep on his right
and the goats on his left." (Matthew 25:32b)
* *I AM: Poems for Expansion and Renewal*

Turning

My college journey

I go to a Christian college in the Midwest, one with a variety of flavors of Christianity, though all of them conservative. (I was taught growing up that "liberal Christians" do not take the Bible seriously.) We take theology courses and go to chapel three times a week. I am fully immersed in Christianity, but a Christianity with more options. I am able to explore a wider set of Christian communities and theologies.

I realize that my conception of God could use some adjusting, and that what I had grown up with wasn't necessarily the whole truth, even though it was proclaimed to be that way. It feels like a relief. I feel much more at home here.

I learn interpretations of Bible verses that make my soul sing with possibility. You mean, men don't have to be the head over women!?! I can care about women's equality and women's rights? (At this time, I still believe that what I believe must come from the Bible, but I am becoming acquainted with more interpretations and more possibilities.)

I'm a part of a college program called Human Needs and Global Resources, and we start learning about colonization around the world. We read Liberation Theology and Henri Nouwen. I spend 6 months in Peru volunteering with Food for the Hungry. I am heartbroken at the thought that there may have been generation after generation of people who didn't know Jesus, and wonder at a God who could condemn them to hell. I wonder if he did in fact do that.

I read and I learn

I read a book about Jesus being our Shepherd. The idea of Jesus being kind and compassionate really speaks to me. This Jesus is patient and able to hold all of my feelings, all of who I am, without any judgment or blame or requiring anything different from me. I don't have to be a certain way to earn his favor or be an acceptable Christian.

I realize that if Jesus is compassionate, he will only speak to me with compassion. I still think I have to listen to Jesus, not myself. But at least I know I only have to listen to the internal voice I hear that's compassionate, and I can weed out the mean and critical voices.

I read a book about prayer where I realize that I can treat God like a real person and talk to him like a real person. My prayers start changing. Instead of using "Christianese," I talk like I would to a friend, and that is nice.

I read about rest and I learn that rest is a valuable part of life. Resting my body, and also resting from constant striving and self-control.

Something is wrong

Something is wrong.
The way I am reacting to this breakup
is messed up.
I can't handle that I hurt him
by ending our relationship.
He is kind and supportive,
but I can't keep going.
My anxiety prevents it.

I'm the one who ends it,
but I can't let it go.
I want to go comfort him, but I can't.
This is agony.
I don't understand why,
but I know something about my reaction is off.
Shouldn't I feel relieved now?

I eventually begin healing, but I still don't know why
that breakup was so hard. All I know is something is
wrong. Something is off. I scour the Christian self-help
books, but don't find an answer. I don't know how to
figure out what's wrong.

Five years later, I start a Masters in Clinical Psychology.

I learn all about
Family systems and inner systems,
non-judgmental styles of relating and listening,
defense mechanisms, and
emotional intelligence.

It's a requirement to go to therapy before you can
become a therapist—
at least at my school, this is a requirement.
So, I go to therapy.

And I learn about my life.
I learn why that breakup was so messy
(codependency).
I learn about my family systems
(codependency there too),
and my internal systems
(a lot of inner critics),
my defense mechanisms,
(rationalization, defensiveness, etc.)
and coping mechanisms,
(perfectionism)
and my emotions
(I don't have to suppress them).

The main verdict:
I am trapped
in a sticky web of
enmeshed relationships.
That's what's wrong.

The breakup was messy
because the relationship was enmeshed,
so when it ended—even though I ended it,
it felt like the end of the world,
like I had fallen into a dark abyss.

I am still struggling to break free

from enmeshment back home
and enmeshment with God.

The beginning of the process
is seeing the sticky web.

The next step is saying
NO!
I'm done with this way of living and relating.

Then comes the slow building of
autonomy, a voice, an independent self,
an independent mind, self-knowing, self-trust,
boundaries, space for my feelings, lots of grief,
and lots of reclamation and celebration.

It starts with seeing.
And welcoming the rising NO within me.

Welcome.

NO

I write NO over and over in huge letters.
NO, NO, NO, NO, NO!!!
It is still hard to say it out loud,
but I can write it and yell it inside.
I feel empowered.
I love the rising NO inside.

I can't make them happy

I can't make them happy.
It isn't possible
without such a level of self-abandonment
and enmeshment
and attunement to their feelings
to make sure I'm doing it just right.
I'll shrivel up inside.

Contemplation and Unraveling

I discover contemplative spiritual practices in my late 20's. A way to connect with God where I can also connect with myself. Ruth Haley Barton's books, Taize (interdenominational singing), and Anglican silent retreats are a lovely taste of this. I spend many years here and feel much more spacious and at rest.

I meet a PCUSA pastor on a dating site. I wonder on our first date if his flavor of Christianity is okay. I visit his church and discover that "liberal" Christians love God too. I learn that the suspicions I have been given of progressive Christians are not true.

This pastor and I get married 3 years later. I find a lot of relief in the PCUSA church. There's no guilt, no intense scrutiny of our inner lives and devotion to God. All questions are allowed and we're supposed to use our minds in knowing God. I like all of this. I don't feel emotionally close to God here though.

When we start a family, we want to be closer to our extended families. We move to my southern hometown to be near my family. I am also now surrounded by the southern brands of spirituality I grew up with. I am especially triggered by Christian radio. I start exploring why. And Christianity begins unraveling for me.

I do tons of research, and contemplation, and therapy. I develop steps to learn self-trust after leaving evangelical subculture. I go from progressive Christian to Christian adjacent.

The final death knell in my centering Christianity is the patriarchy and hierarchy baked into the forms I see of Christianity. I cannot support hierarchy in my spirituality. I continue to like Jesus, an advocate and teacher who didn't fit into anyone's boxes.

I find Internal Family Systems therapy, and create harmony and healing in my internal world. Through this healing and internal harmony, I am able to reconnect to myself, and thus to the divine that I knew implicitly as a young child.

Clues

What I think
what I feel
what I want

clues!
these are clues

I can treasure them
and see them for what they are
embrace them
as message-givers

They are loud and luminous
quiet and caring
full of foreboding
or humming with joyful anticipation

They are

What I think
what I feel
what I want

They teach me a game

They teach me a game
called Christian religion.
I wonder if they know it is a game.
They tell me it is
Truth
Life or Death
Everything.
I don't know they are lying.
Do they know they are lying?

It's not till after I leave that I see the games.
There are lots of games within the game.
I'm just trying to spot them now.
Let's see if we can come up with some of them:

The In-or-out-of-Heaven game: if you're lost, or
backslidden, or a hypocrite, you lose and you're out.
Some additional rules in other groups: if you don't speak
in tongues, if you're not baptized, if you're not born
again, if you're not a Republican…

The In-or-out-of-Favor game: if you don't do your
devotions, if you don't pray enough, if you sin, if you
don't ask for forgiveness, if you don't forgive, if you
don't tithe, etc. you are out of god's favor and the
church's favor. But we're willing to take you back if you
repent.

The spiritual bypassing game: see how many
bypassing phrases you can learn and use them as often as

possible. You get a point every time you use one. Here are some I learn:

·   God is good all the time. All the time, God is good.

·   God won't give you more than you can handle.

·   God is testing you to see if he can trust you.

The Christian witness game: learn as many witnessing tactics as you can, and use at least 1 every time you encounter a non-Christian. Remember their mortal soul is at stake! And don't forget "you may be the only bible some people read" so be on your best Christian behavior at all times. Take a point away (or a soul away from heaven) every time you slip up!

Okay, I'm getting triggered now, so I'm gonna leave it at that.

These games do not feel like games to me.
They feel like life or death.
I internalize them.
I ingest them.
I breathe them in and hold my breath so I can hopefully succeed.

I don't like it

I don't like your rules.
I don't want to play your game.

Why not?
You afraid?

I didn't know you were a bully until I said no.

Stupid rules

stupid
stupid
stupid
stupid
stupid rules.

who made these stupid rules?

Taking Up Space

I don't appreciate you misunderstanding and mislabeling
my persistent demand for autonomy as
…belligerent
…strongwilled
…rebellious
…ungrateful
…disobedient.

I am in need of myself
Don't take it away from me!
Don't ask that of me!

Don't ask me to cut that off
Don't tell me to excavate myself
Don't demand agreement, or keep pushing until you get
it.
DON'T!

What you are trying to take from me is not unruly,
disobedient, sinful behavior, but my very self. You are
communicating that I am not acceptable unless…
I am quiet
submissive
patient, and
putting your feelings first.

I hate that you don't have space to see me.
You say you love me, but
you can't see me.
You can't.

Until now, I have had autonomy through separating.
Creating my own space.
Regrowing myself inside from the squashed seeds and
mounded, impacted, parched, unnourished earth.
Nourishing, watering, singing, chanting, loving, resting,
waiting, regulating, co-creating
into a lush, spacious, enchanting, exhilarating, rest-filled,
soul-soaked, magical place.

And it is time.
My teenager says it's time.
To take up that space
in relationships too.
Courageously
unapologetically
lovingly
assertively
me.

Love, in theory

love does not:

dismiss me
(while telling me you value me)

override me
(while telling me you're listening)

force me to change
(while telling me you accept and love me no matter
what)

expect me to comply
(in order for you to feel okay about me and us)

silence me
(while telling me you value my voice)

push me to agree with you
(while telling me you value my opinion)

take things personally
(while telling me you want to hear what I have to say)

pressure me to talk to you
(while telling me you've always valued my autonomy)

gaslight me
(see above list)

in theory you love me.
but in those moments you are not loving me.

It is by knowing

It is by knowing myself
          that I can know you

It is by accepting myself
          that I can accept you

It is by making space for myself
          that I can make space for you

It is by being
          myself
               that I can let you be
                         yourself

In case you were still wondering…

It is not by repressing myself
          that I can know you

It is not by judging myself
          that I can accept you

It is not by being small
          that I can make space for you

It is not by denying myself
          that I can let you be yourself

And in the event that you are skeptical or don't agree,
I'll make myself even clearer...

I will not deny and sacrifice myself

because you tell me it is noble,

and good, and selfless

I will not judge, control, or manage myself
        so I can be acceptable to you

I will not be small
        because you imply I'm too much (for you)

I am just the right size

A Demanding God

The God I was taught—
The immutable, invisible, omnipresent, omnipotent
Father God of Heaven and Earth—
Was a force to be reckoned with,
A force to be feared.
More than a force - a god in the image of an Imperial
Man.

Always saying, "not enough"—
Do more - pray more, repent more, evangelize more.

Always the threat of torment, of separation, of
abandonment,
Pressing from above.
The pressure was wrapped with words of "love"

As it insisted on:
Devotion, Adoration, Worship
Without ceasing.

And demanded:
Obedience, Conformity, Compliance, Submission, and
Self-Sacrifice.

It commanded:
Thou Shalt Not
And tried to consume, and punish, and shame my life-
force out of me.

It tried to take me from myself, and replace me with
itself.
In the name of "saving my soul" it tried to violently take
it from me.

The Escape

I escape.
And return to Myself.
As I heal, I find life in Myself
and celebrate that Life.
I no longer have to question it,
shame myself for it,
or exile it for fear it could be crushed or stolen.
I am Myself
And I am Whole.

There is more to the story

For many years,
I followed all the rules
that Christian patriarchy gave me
wrapped in the gift wrap called "family values."
I didn't know there was another choice,
another way to see,
another path to take.

It was supposed to protect me and make me a holy
person.
Or that's what I was told.

Instead,
it made me a shell of a person
too small and weak to protest.

And I was one of the "lucky ones"
—At least I was white,
and wanted to marry a man,
so I got applause and status for what I gave up.

Others who could never mark their purity ruler "white"
were subjugated and oppressed
inside and out.

Land taken,
families separated,
lives ended after torture
in the name of discipline,
law and order,

god's order,
and "civilized" living.

And if your sexuality did not align—
could not,
would not,
conform
to the extreme binaries of
submissive woman
or lone ranger man,
you were shunned,
shamed,
jailed,
and denied basic human rights.

Now I know there is another way,
There is more to the story than what I was told.
I have healed and nourished myself back to wholeness.
I have been learning the ancient ways of recently bruised
peoples,
and I stand with them.
I will not tolerate ideologies, worldviews, and laws
disguised as gifts,
that are really instruments of torture, control, and death.

Together we rise,
We sing, we chant,
It is not the end.
We will overcome.*

---

* *I AM: Poems for Expansion and Renewal*

Prayer is not a transaction

Prayer is not a transaction:
Something I
Ask for,
Plead for,
Beg for,

And wait for an answer…

I wonder will I ever get one?

Maybe…
if I see the outcome I wanted
Or maybe I see nothing.

And then my faith in god is dependent on that,
my hope for what happens is dependent on that

Sending it out into the netherworld
to a god that I've been told is a certain way
but not because
I've experienced god that way, but
just because I've been told god is that way

It's a very strange way to relate.
We're told it's not supposed to be a transaction
but how can it be otherwise?
How can we actually listen (and hear something)
in the way we're told to listen?
We're supposed to listen for a still small voice,
an inner resonance

but what if we don't have that, what then?

And if we have too much
Voice
then we're called crazy
and filled with a demon;
seeing visions is hallucinating,
you can't trust dreams
But you can trust "the Words of God" as we give them to
you...
Then who am I listening to?
You
Or god?

How is anyone supposed to see or hear or know god
in such a rigid, small way?

My prayer is not
a transaction
anymore.

My prayer is my life
my prayer is me
Being
in the world
and listening
to the wave
and the particle

Seeing the different ways
one scene
looks

in a different light

Seeing the
Moon
and the stars;
The moon's courses
change and shift

Inside—
and on the Shore,
Holding me…
to the Earth
Holding me…
and gently swaying
Rocking me like a mother rocks
her children
and also standing
Still
A great foundation
that never moved
beneath the weight of my body
resting, playing, loving, living

Prayer is not a transaction.
Prayer is life
Prayer is breath
Prayer is me
in Life.*

---

* *I AM: Poems for Expansion and Renewal*

Kicking original sin to the curb

I have less and less tolerance for the theology of original sin, total depravity, and penal substitutionary atonement. Because this theology absolutely screwed me over. It told me I had to abandon, control, and even sometimes punish myself in order to be safe. These teachings told me lies about myself, and then told me, don't worry, there is good news - that a loving *(ahem, narcissistic)* god could save me. That he deigned to love me and adopt me back into his family even though I didn't deserve one shred of his kindness. (But if I didn't live 100% sold out to him without any piece of myself left, he would vomit me out of his mouth, and tell me to go away with the goats into hell.)

This may feel like a major part of your religious screw over too, or it might not. There are plenty of other messed up hurtful things happening.

Expansion

why do you search for god out there?
for transcendence?

and in the process cut off the ability to see
and be a part of immanence
right here

instead you spend your time proving
and parsing
searching for a reality
for a god
beyond our knowing and our grasp

looking
learning
longing
navel-gazing
searching for reasons why you can't hear god

and all the time god is whispering
all around us
can you listen for immanence?
can you look around you at the divine
can you receive it
and restore that connection

instead of cutting yourself off
from all that is this world
in search of something else

can you receive what is here?
can you be a part of the divine here
all that is within you and around you
speaking words of freedom
and truth and life
I found a well-spring—
it's inside
the well-spring that I heard would come from outside,
from the holy spirit
and I found it inside
I found it through the earth
through immanence
through knowing and being connected to myself:
       trusting myself (not distrusting)
       loving myself (not second-guessing)
       knowing myself (not avoiding myself).
knowing myself is the greatest doorway to knowing
others
and the divine

if you can't be in self
you can't be connected to anything else

all that's left is
pleading
hoping
longing
desperation…
for something that is already inside you
(that you were told to look for outside of you)

that empty hole

that I was told is a god-shaped hole that only god can
fill;
it's You—
you already have it inside.
cast off the burdens
—as jesus said—
and I will give you rest.
yes, I know jesus
he's with me
he never left me

he loves that I drink of this water every day
and that it's new and fresh and renewing
and I am there too
I am the life
I am my life
I am my only life
and jesus is with me
jesus is with me in my life
jesus loves me and my life
jesus loves me the way I am
and who I am

we were made from expansion
from a tiny little seed
speck, dot
big bang if you will that kept exploding and expanding
in energy and colors
vibrance and life

all we do now is try to cultivate

squash it
control it
excavate it

what if we let it expand
what if we let it be reborn
what if there is more life here than we realized
and more hope for us
what if we step out of the way
and listen
then we may hear our path forward*

---

* *I AM: Poems for Expansion and Renewal*

God

The term "God" sometimes works for me
And sometimes doesn't

"God" is so laced with
The patriarchy:
A male
Ruler
In the sky

Sometimes I make the letters small
—god—
So I know she is universal
With and among
Not
Over

But really,
I like other words better
Expansive words
With and among and within me words

Words like...
Life
Flow
Universe
Divine She
The Divine We
Non-binary and both together
All the colors of the rainbow
Spread out we are a color wheel of beauty

Contained in One
Contained in All
Not contained at all
We are One*

_____

* *I AM: Poems for Expansion and Renewal*

Eden

I am eden. we all are eden.

Torn

I forgot what it felt like to be torn
between what "god said"
and what I felt inside
between what my parents said or implied
and what I wanted

then it became between
what my parents wanted and what someone else wanted,
a boyfriend perhaps
i was so unfamiliar and unpracticed at that point at
listening to myself
that autonomy wasn't first breaking away by listening to
myself
it was feeling torn between my parents and a fiance

more recently it was feeling torn between
my mom wanting me to be a stay-at-home mom
and my husband wanting me to work and make money
what did I want?
I felt so aware of their strong feelings pulling me
like a tug of rope game
who will win?
it took a lot of work to get enough emotional space to
explore what I wanted

Finding My Voice

my words
so rich inside
delicious
dark
deep
bottomless
like cavernous riches

sometimes…
dark, hard, bitter and brittle, easy-to-break

sometimes…
fiery and indignant
yelling…
roaring…
rolling…
   like a drumroll that will not be silenced
vibrating…
   like a deep, earth-filled rumble
you will not!
I will not let you!
you cannot and will not!
I will not let you!

sometimes…
spicy, smooth, and sensual like Nora Jones singing her
jazz

sometimes…
they meet my lips

and share their riches

sometimes…
they meet my fingers
and find their way onto a page

sometimes…
they meet my arms
in a tight hug

always…
they belong to me
and nourish me.

A Feminist Manifesto

We will not
be...
suppressed
subdued
overlooked
overused
misused
abused
used at all

We will not...
repress
apologize
shrink
deny
sacrifice
look away

We will...
rekindle
renew
refresh
expand
express
EXHALE
ground
center
hold our sovereign space
live in our bodies
love our bodies

know our power
embody our power
love our power
be our power
be ourselves

Exclusionary Joy

I chose joy to the exclusion of all other feelings for years
upon years upon years.
My bones feel weary of this forced joy.
This exclusionary joy.

Exclusionary,
Just like only some types of people are acceptable,
only our beliefs are okay,
only god-directed thoughts are permitted,
only specific emotions are admissible (and not labeled
emotions at all, because emotions, like anything from the
body, is untrustworthy and base; however fruits of the
spirit are praiseworthy and desirable) ,
only certain genders and sexualities allowed,
only certain roles admired,
only thin body-types not shamed,
only productive minds and bodies praised…

only, only, only.

I am rewatching Inside Out with my two kids.
And it shows so well what happens when only joy is
allowed.
Everything falls apart.*
You grow numb and unfeeling
because you don't have other feelings to help you
navigate hard things in life,
where joy is a cover-up, a mask, a survival-tactic.

---

* This is an allusion to Chinua Achebe's book *Things Fall Apart.*

I'm still drawn to joy. But it feels more like awe, wonder, self-compassion, inspiration, being known and loved for who I am without a joy-mask. Without forced joy trying to push through my veins and bones willing me to feel, exude, and show the "joy of the lord."

I don't, I can't choose joy. It chooses and finds me, in the deep well of warmth and well-being. The sun at my center. The warmth of love and being and belonging.

The tragedy

I was told that if I looked inside,
I would find something rotten,
sinful at its core.
Always doomed to lead me astray.

Never look inside unless you want to feel guilt & conviction,
so you can repent.
Once you repent, still don't look inside. It's dangerous. It
could lead you astray.
It could mean you're taking your eyes off of God and making
yourself an idol.

Open the door of your heart to let Jesus in, but don't look
around. Leave real fast and praise God for wanting to have
mercy on you.

The tragedy is:
I was told I was the enemy.
I was worthless apart from God.
I could never trust myself.

The Good News

The good news is:
When I actually looked inside, I found something different
I found a scared kid who was so afraid of hurting others.
I found a caregiver and rescuer trying so hard to help others
who were hurting.
I found a perfectionist trying so hard to do it all right.
I found a taskmaster, laying down the godly rules and pushing
others to obey.
I found a scavenger, scanning for emotional food to fill her
up.
I found a fixer, always trying to make herself and everything
else better.

And I found that they all loved me. And I loved them.
We could heal the separation,
Release the heavy burdens,
And renew the inner compass at my core.
The spark of playfulness and life.

Where the Wild Things Are

Part 1: Frozen smile

I have a smile
plastered on my face.
Always
be friendly
be cheerful
be helpful
be godly
be good.

I am told
that there are lots of scary things
and people in this world.

Monsters
Strangers
Strange things
Suspicious things

so always be ready
to give a defense for
the light within you
and be wary of the dark
out there.

Push out
push away
denounce
deny

74

distance
from any association
with the Wild Things.

They are uncivilized
uncolonized
unwashed
unsaved
fleshly and flesh-eating
wild
monsters.

Send them away.
We are the good
ones.
The godly
ones.
The righteous
ones.
Only one Savior.
Only one Way.
Stay in the Light.

In short, children,
we are good
and they are dangerous.

Part 2: The robot

I have been
colonized.
I have obeyed.

I have scoured
my inner world
and sent away
any part of me
that did not fit,
did not conform.

I am a robot
of a person.
Now I am
good enough
to stay in the
family,
culture,
community.
I am safe.

Part 3: The voyage

The un-colonized
un-conditioned
pre-conditioned
parts of me

76

are sent away
on a long voyage
to a lost island

and left
alone.

They do their best
to survive.
They huddle together for warmth
and build shelter
and love.

But they also know
they
are
exiles.

And
they
are
alone.

Part 4: Lifeless

I cannot
bear to be
a robot
any longer.

I am
lifeless
and
listless
and
helpless.

Part 5: Ray of Wildness

A ray of wildness
breaks through.

A whiff of what
it feels like to be
human.

I must find the
wild things.

I must find me.

Part 6: Soma

On my sea-journey
I begin feeling.

First
the rhythmic
oceanic depths
break the calm surface

in a rumba with the air
to the cadence of the moon

The endarkenment
of a body full of,
well,
shiny robot-parts,
that slowly become
soft
soma,
sprayed with,
healed by,
and buoyed on
the salty depths.

My body becomes ready
to find the wild parts
left on the wild
island alone.

Part 7: The Reunion

I see them!
I cry.
They are not monsters,
but little children,
tender and helpless.
Wild in their manners,
which I adore.

I am here!
I cry.
We cry.
We laugh.
I hold them tight.
They embrace me.
And melt the last
of the robot
away.

We hold a funeral
for the robot
there on that island.

The robot tried so hard.
It was so good,
we say.

I hated it.
It sent me away.
It thought I was no good.
The little ones say.

You are right.
We say.
You are just right.
We say.

You are home
with us.
We say.

The Rabbit Hole

I escaped from a world without curiosity

I escaped from a top-down world
to a delightful topsy-turvy one.

From a world without curiosity to Alice's Wonder-land.

From a world of black and white
(where white is on the top of the top-down way to be).

First I found a world of grey between the black and
white, but
was so conditioned to be wary of colorful people,
that I had to watch for a bit
before I could approach the rabbit hole.

And, oh, how glad I am I did.

I found myself back where I started
in my home world.

I escaped from a world not made for me
to one where I belong.

I discovered
magical realism
buried in a rabbit hole.

The Curtain

Now I know that what I feared
is just
a scared old man
hiding behind a green
                    curtain
in a green
            city.

I do not have to
fear
        him.
Or myself.

It is Done

I let it go.
It is time.
It is necessary.
There is nothing left for me there.
I both grieve and rejoice at its passing.
It was a large part of my life,
and it needs to be over.

It wafts by every now and then
and I take in its scent.
The remembrance of something
that no longer exists for me.
I pause,
and I mark the moment,
mark the entity's significance in my life.

If I keep it at a distance,
I can recollect with nostalgia,
but when the details reappear,
my heart races,
and my body becomes the site
of a state of flight.
The desire,
the urge,
the necessity of getting away,
becomes noisy
and insistent.

I step back again.
I know it is done.

It is no longer mine.
No longer my place or my identity.
I am free of its clutches,
of its claims on my soul.

Christianity for me
is a thing of the past.

I attempted to remove the thorns,
but the roses buried me in their overbearing fragrance,
and pulled their branches around me,
trying to turn me into a piece of rose bush,
attempting to bury me in its tight embrace,
so I have buried it for myself instead.

I see others enjoy the rose-bush with autonomy and
equanimity
and I rejoice for them, even as I know it is over for me.

The door

i want what is on the other side of that door
it is beckoning to me
the unknown feels delicious
exciting
crisp and calling

Liberation

I flipped the switch.
A new existence twinkled at me.

I stepped across to meet it.

Ahhh, escaped my body,
the relief
of self-liberation.

I stepped
out
of the ill-fitting cosmology
of christianity.

And stepped over the threshold
into Gaia's embrace.

The twinkle of stars met me
on the darkest day of the year.
New and ancient kin reacquainted.

On the other side,
I found myself in my own body and knowing.

No longer watching myself,
contorting myself
to fit into a colonized body.

No longer contorting
my beliefs

to support colonizers making me
 their prey.

That light is out.
Extinguished.
I no longer have to watch my insides flee or be devoured
by shame.

I am no longer a colonized body
in a colonized world.

I am free.
I am in me.
My skin feels warm
and welcoming.
My body rises to greet me
with a warm embrace.
I have come home
again.

My life appears to be a journey
of coming home
again and again.

My body is safe.
My body is good.
It is my home.
It is just the right size and shape
for me.

It doesn't have to fit anyone else.
It is mine.

It does have to struggle living in a world
that does not have a light switch to flip.
But I can be a twinkle.

My compass

My compass used to be
authority
do right
be right
make everyone happy
follow the godly rules.

I knew if I stepped out of line,
 because I felt:
shame
anxiety
dread
fear (of rejection and separation)

I learned that this did not lead to life
so it could not be right.
Shame and anxiety were not "conviction" - they were
tools to keep me obedient.

I learned to find a life-giving compass
one that said ah-ha!
here is:
life
freedom
expansion
rest
delight
ahhh.

That is my compass. That leads to life.

Safe to See

I can see many things that I couldn't before. Because it's safe to look, to ask, to question, to inquire, to investigate, to explore, to be curious.

And I choose:
Well-being over success
Rest over over-productivity
Being real over being perfect
Self-advocacy over self-abnegation
Assertiveness over niceness

There are other things that may still be shrouded in illusion.
Or in mystery?

I Just Am

I don't have to defend myself
I just Am.
I am the way an apple is (juicy and sweet)
A snake is (it doesn't know it's a symbol of divinity)
A leaf is (fragile and supple all at the same time)
The sunshine is (warm and inviting)

I had this revelation
Like a thunderclap
 Or was it a warm breeze?
If I don't have to defend god,
I don't have to defend me either.
Well, look at that.

Something New

New has so many possibilities…

New relationships - with myself, with my body, with the earth, with other spiritual seekers

New way of responding - assertiveness not people-pleasing, expressing rather than absorbing, questioning rather than explaining myself

New way of being - connected to all of myself
New values - self-trust, self-advocacy, activism, liberation

New worldview - based on well-being of each of us that supports each other in community (not starting from a list handed to me of what to believe about god, myself, my family, "the world", my mission, my value, my relationships, my country, the systems around me, etc.)

New vision and energy

New understanding of how my brain, nervous system, and body work in a neurodivergent body

New conflicts with old relationships that aren't used to the new

New little humans in my daily life and love

New things they're learning all the time

New ways they see the world

New pieces of self they are discovering and sharing with us

The Dance is Different

It is interesting what happens as I release my need to create a good response from you. When that no longer is my compass.

I do not need your smile, or fear your frown of disapproval.

I already know: I am good and I am worthy.

I feel lighter and free-er and fuller. Standing arms-wide with the wind.

I am on the edge of the unknown—a great and vast mystery, a grand adventure unfolding before me.

I know how to chart my course. How to listen inside and wayfind my way.

But I do not know how to relate to you anymore. The dance is different.

I'm no longer taking responsibility for your subterranean emotional noise. I am living my authenticity...but it finds no echo back, no welcoming response. Only your frozen skin trying to figure out what to do. This is a new place for us both.

When I Trust you to Know
What's Best For You

I
trust
you.

I don't have to decide
if what you say is
true,

if I condone it,
or not.

if I agree,
or not.

Listening does not require
approval.

I am not here to judge the merits of your case.
How sad, that I was taught to do that very thing.

I was taught
To spend every conversation
either signaling my belief in God,
or reading others' signals.

I was taught
To listen if what they said
stood up to what the Bible said.

True or not true.
Approve or disapprove.

So much hypervigilance,
hyperawareness,
hyperalertness,
in every conversation.

It is peaceful,
this trusting thing.
I can trust you to mean what you say.
I don't have to dig into it for hidden meanings or signals.

I can trust you to know what's best for you.
I don't have to jump in with instructions or judgments,
corrections for "my brother in Christ."

How awful that was.

This trusting thing,
it is good.
And I approve.

Healing

Reclaiming the Prayer

I want to go back
Really, I have gone back
inside
To tell the young girl
The me-girl
who was on her knees

Asking Jesus to come into her heart
With all the earnestness she had
(after the shock wore off
that she was told she was bad
And didn't know god after all
"You're sinful" he says
And god can't be near you
Unless you pray the prayer
I give you)

That the man that told you that—was bad
And actually, you just found out your parents thought so
too
But they didn't tell you for some reason
They didn't tell you
they didn't like him
And he made them
uncomfortable

Why is that you wonder?
They didn't think it affected
you?
They thought it was something to Celebrate,

Even though
They didn't like
How
he
told
you
"The good news"

It was still supposedly "good news"

Really,
It feels like what happened was
You stopped…
Listening
To
Yourself

You
Started…
Managing
Yourself

You only listened to
The
Words
The church
Told you

The Way
The Truth
The Life
They say - we know the way - only this way!

A certain way
To read
The bible
A certain way
To hear God
To know God
To talk about God

You had to live according to those ways
Make sure
God
Was on
Your side
And close to you
At all times

It was hard
It was a lot of pressure

And it didn't have anything to do with god

The Divine was in you all the time
The Divine Feminine no one spoke of
The Goddess
Who has been excluded
She is you
She knows you
She speaks your name

Now I know
My heart was always hers
Because it's Mine

102

The weight of the world

I see you there in biology class
Reading your Bible so you can be a witness to the light
Trying to hard
Wanting so earnestly…
What exactly?
Their salvation, them to know Jesus?
…also to just be me and put this weight down
And that to be okay
That the weight of the world didn't have to rest on my shoulders
The weight of their eternal fate up to me to influence
Oh, that in itself is coercive marketing.
Name brand placement in a classroom. Jesus here.
Taking your campus for Christ, that was the phrase wasn't it?
Take all of us captive for Christ
No wonder I felt like a hostage inside for so long trying to take others hostage to "the light", the "true way"

Put down the weight*…

---

* *Put down the weight of your aloneness and ease into the conversation. The kettle is singing even as it pours you a drink, the cooking pots have left their arrogant aloofness and seen the good in you at last. All the birds and creatures of the world are unutterably themselves. Everything is waiting for you.* (Excerpt from "Everything is Waiting" for You by David Whyte)

Somatic healing

During my massage today,
I was reborn.
Nails loosening in my back.
Layers of thin wood, plywood,
so thin they are like a pastry,
coming off.

There were treasures hidden away.
Hidden for me—
inside the fascia, and tendons, and muscles.
My body hid them away.

And now, the intruder burden is lifting
and I have them back.
My humanity and my divinity.

***

The tension in my body,
kept me taught like a rope,
tied in a shipyard knot.

I thought it was armor.
Maybe some of it was (and is).
But some of it was a burden.

A burden I don't have to carry any longer.

This weighty burden
started coming off—

like a cape flowing behind me,
with space for the air to flow through.

Thicker than fabric,
textured, and heavy, like plywood,
whisper-thin like pastry,
the layers started separating
and pulling away.

There were nails
in my shoulders
keeping them in place.
They creaked loose
and began evacuating as well.

It appears someone tried to build a house on my back.
Not on shifting sand, or rock...
on.my.back.

They laid the burden of the whole world there,
Atlas-style,
nailing it in for good measure.
Sealing all the layers,
and covering it all with invisible paint.

Body Language

It's taken a while to learn this language, of
yes vs. no,
I like it vs. I don't like it,
It's for me vs. it's not for me,
It's mine to do vs. It's not mine.

First, I needed
permission inside
to listen.
To listen to myself
and what my body was telling me.

I learned that my body is my guide.
My compass to safety, pleasure, rest, balance,
wholeness…
all the things.

Then, I started learning the language.
What do I feel like when I think of my favorite food—an
easy yes
Oh, this subtle opening inside, anticipation, openness.

It's Ironic

it's ironic
and amazing
that coming home to yourself
trusting yourself
isn't an act of rugged individualism.
it's a level of autonomy
that allows you to live
fully and completely
inside of yourself
and
naturally connect to all of life—
you are not isolated,
but actually more connected
by connecting to yourself,
you are reconnecting with the
mycelium of life.

I let go

I release the burden of making sure I don't hurt anyone - intentionally or unintentionally.

There used to be a constant awareness of others' emotions, and a monitoring and censoring of my actions and words.

How did my words land? How did they react?

I must be the hero, the good one, the responsible one, the considerate one, the receptive one, the kind one, the generous one, the understanding one. I must be it, and others must see it.

This one way of being in my body and in the world is too confining and soul-draining. I am learning that my nervous system can have ease. It does not have to appease. All can be at rest.

I have a wall of armor allowing emotions in, but no emotions out. The armor is still afraid I'm dangerous. The wall is afraid I will hurt others if I let out what I've held for so long.

My anger will come out hot and fast like a dragon blast. I can see a blaze of fire coming out of the dragon in my middle. The anger must come out. It is the only way to metabolize it. It is the only way to balance the system.

We've been on the precarious foundation of flight, freeze, and appease for so long. Hold it in, run away, make it better.

Now it's time to let it out. And I don't want it to hurt those closest to me.

Let me be me. Value me for me. Celebrate me. Support me. Don't tell me what to do, ask me what I need. I need rest baked into the day. Time alone, time to think, to write, to be. Time to not be needed and not need to do. Time to move, time to be in nature. And time to connect.

Now I know that repair is possible. I did not know that when flight, freeze, and appease were my go-to choices for so much of my life. I don't want to cause dirty pain, unjust pain, the result of my need to let out pent-up, stuffed down thoughts and feelings that the person doesn't deserve. Clean pain of confrontation is good. And necessary, but takes a lot of energy and effort.

I don't want to have to be the mediator. I don't want to have to be the level-headed one. I don't want to have to move into a presenter part. Is there an assertive part or an assertive skill for all my parts to express rather than present, but turn the intensity level and clarity level to the most helpful markers?

I just want to yell. To yell and yell and yell. With my whole body. From the middle of me. I guess that's my sacral area. That's where the dragon is. Yell and yell and yell. Until it is enough.

This is the time I am letting go.
Of needed to do it right.
Of censoring myself.
Of doing the work of managing everyone else's
emotions and responses, or possible emotions or
responses.
I am just yelling.
Until I'm done.

Dangerous

am I dangerous?
why yes I am.
I am dangerous
because you can't control me.
you can't make me feel ashamed.
you can't put me back in the good girl box.
I am here and I am me.
All of me.
I do not live by your rules anymore.
I do not live by your judgments.
I do not live by the fear you tried to embed in me.
So don't try to limit me or make me smaller.
Or tell me that being me is somehow bad.
I know me. And I know I am only dangerous in a very
good way.
So watch out world.
I am dangerous
and I am here.

My Emotions Speak

Listen.
Listen.
Listen.

My emotions are crying out: listen.
The only way is to listen.
If you want to survive, you must
listen—

I open my ears, and
my emotions speak to me:

> Don't run from us,
> don't push us down,
> don't swallow us,
> in hopes we'll go away.
>
> We cannot.
> Until we do our magic.
> Until we alchemize your pain..
> We are your salve,
> not an extra burden.
> We are the way through.
> We are your way through.
>
> Release us slowly
> and we will heal you.
> We will ferry you across.
> Only then can you leave what happened behind.
> And find respite on the other shore.

We are your guides,
not sherpas.
We cannot carry the pain burden,
but we will show you the way.
We are your way to the other side.

I slowly learn
    to be taught
and guided
by my emotions.

I learn to be fiercely and tenderly present
to my pain,
to others' pain,
without taking it in.

I feel healthier and stronger
more full of myself,
thankful for my guides.

Where the Lost Things Go

There is a preschool part of me who knows how to cross her arms and put her foot down. Who is not afraid to know how she feels. Not afraid to show how she feels.

I love this fierce part of me. I love her and I need her. She got kicked down to the basement of my inner world, and it is time to find her and bring her home.

I approach. Her arms are crossed and there is a determined look on her face.

She demands:
How could you? How could you shove me down there in the basement?

I reply:
I was afraid. I love your fierceness. Other people didn't love it and I didn't know what else to do. I'm so sorry.

Inner Nourishment

I am naturally attuned to needs—
my needs and the needs of others.

With the blessing of my upbringing,
I went through my white savior stage,
trying to codependently rescue everyone else.
I was taught to be self-sacrificial, and I obeyed.
I saw a need, and I tried to meet it, no matter the cost to
myself.
I felt desperation trying to get anyone else to care, and to
help me.

I learned.
It took a long time, but
I learned to respectfully support others
without taking on their pain as my own.

I learned how to care for myself
rather than abandon myself through self-sacrifice.

I know how to relate to myself now,
regarding needs:
Find a need, and meet it.
Be compassionate with myself about my needs.
Expand what constitutes a need,
rather than relegating it to a preference.
Listen to myself when I'm getting stretched thin,
and care for myself, give myself breathing room.

The next portal awaits.

The sign just lit up above the door:
SELF-GENEROSITY.
This is mind-blowing.
To be *generous* with myself.
As I try to wrap my mind around this,
I'm all out of words.
Generous.
I try out other words and phrases to help me understand:
Lavish—no.
Abundance—sort-of.
Kind—not quite.
I try the thesaurus…
Open-handed—getting there.
Liberal—lots of connotations, but I like it.
Big-hearted—that comes closest.
I'm still at a loss for words.
But I do have feelings.
This warmth in my heart towards myself.
This sense of the Goddesses of Enough
teaching me that I don't have to live in "just-barely-
enoughness"
And I'm laughing because this message
is coming in the midst of a fascist takeover,
where everything feels like scarcity is looming
and scarcity is a reality.

I think this is my food,
my nourishment,
during these lean times.
Inside is an abundant picnic
while lounging at an outdoor concert.
Outside may be a wasteland,

but inside is enough.
Inside of me is
generous.

The Awakening

The slow awakening begins.
The healing and thawing and calling forth.

All I know is the realm of her protectors:
Body armor so strong it holds me together,
just beneath a friendly, accommodating exterior.

My body holds us,
So I can survive without her.
And she can be shielded from detection.

From the deep recesses she has been calling,
with a language I didn't understand.

The voice of limbs and organs and fascia,
of sinuses and histamines and lung constriction.
I feel her desperation in each body blow.
*Fix it now. It's too much. Who has the answer? Who can
help us?*

That body is ready to be known,
and released,
from the job as sole sentinel over my safety.
The armor morphs into a skin-suit, and…

She emerges.
We can be one again.
She is released with a flood of tears,
the protectors tell my body it is over;
we can find rest.

I am not in scarcity

I am in solidarity

I am no longer living in scarcity and desperation, pleading with god to answer my prayers. hoping the fervency and frequency will show him how much i care, will sway him to answer.

please, please, God, heal him. you are a mighty God. please hear us and have mercy on him. please. please. please. (cue desperation and pleading)
we need your presence, show us your favor. we don't deserve you. fill us up, god. we need you. we are nothing without you. please, god.

I am in living in solidarity, sturdiness, and presence.

I am not trying to be grateful (while feeling desperately helpless and disappointed)
I am not trying at all.

I am being.
I am present.

I have agency.
I have impact.
I know I matter.

I am connected to all that is living
and life-giving:
the life-generating

and regenerating,
composting and seeding,
nourishing richness of the soil
keeping the seeds in cool cozy care
until it's time for them to poke their heads up
and see the world

Baby bird

I am like a baby bird these days
mouth wide open,
hungry,
but not for physical food.
For soul nourishment,
a new way to see.
Teach me this new way,
this new way for me,
but really the Ancient Ways:
The Wisdom of
First
Peoples
and Mother Earth
and Wisdom
Herself.

My soul is malnourished
from consuming
and never being satisfied;
Striving,
and never finding the finish line,
or rest.
I am worn out
from being in the world
and not of it.

The world - this earth -
is my road home:
to belonging,
and knowing,

and connection.
Giving and receiving
the ebb and flow of
Life.

I am returning
to wonder
to my home
to myself
to my kin.

And they receive me;
but they also need healing.
They have been trampled,
and "tamed,"
depleted and consumed.

They need me as much as I need them.*

---

* *I AM: Poems for Expansion and Renewal*

A New Story

I need a new story.
A new beginning.
New imaginings of the ancient ways.
And the first days - the first cycles of sunlight and moonlight.
I do not trace my ancestors and heritage to Adam and Eve, to a garden of misogyny, betrayal, shame, and exile.
I have connected to myself and the earth in the here and now. I feel the vibrations and my place.
I am me.
I already am.
I have been.
I am awake for the mysteries that will be unveiled.
But the tether to the past, through my ancestors, is unclear.
The prophecy of the future is coming.
The past
Leaning into our past
Will help us and connect us to our present and our future.

The Mountain

crunch, crunch, snap
inhale, exhale
lift, lower, lift, lower
expanding lungs
expelling air
crisp coolness
sunsplashes
swaths of shade
wooded paths
inclined
to meet the pinnacle.

I have arrived.
welcoming vistas
greet my wonder.
I breathe rejuvenation
as awe bounds up to see
                              over
                          the
                              edge
of the world.

***

In another life
another mountain,
it was all different:
sworded plants grabbed at me
ripping and shredding:
"you can't have it."

124

you must die.
you don't deserve.
it will be taken
    if you don't—surrender,
relinquish,
give up
your life,
and praise the
Maker.

The Maker
owns this mountain
and the world.
You must submit and praise.
Serve and self-punish.
Only then will you be spared.
Do not think a thought he
would not consider a gift.
All thoughts, and feelings,
and actions, and intentions
must be gifts to the Maker.

***

I am the Mountain.

The Mountain is with
    and within
             and without.
        My breath.
      My view.
My form.

From her summit, crisp
clarity fills my lungs and sight.

The Mountain is my kin.

I find her heartbeat
as I rest on her rugged, loamy soil.
I feel her vibrations deep to her core,
        like a purring tiger, fiercely content.
I rest on her surface after
    traveling the deepest recesses of her labyrinthine
caves.
shedding all of the Maker's marks,
                                messages,
                                    and molds...
until I was free and unformed.
until I found myself
and knew myself again.

From her cosmic core,
I restored my center, and found my dwelling,
        among my kin.
I recognize them, I know them,
I belong.
I am known and beloved.
I am home.

Coming Home

I'm doing the work
The work of coming home

I've cleared out all of the
Shrapnel
The wounds
They've been tended to and healed

And now we are calling in
and reclaiming
all the parts that have wandered and are coming home
I'm so glad you're here

I'm finding myself
And knowing myself
For the first time
And everytime
And before time
And this time

I am myself
And I am home

Home

I am home

I am home
I can't say I wandered far away

More like…
Parts of me were missing

They got
Stuffed down
Shoved in a closet
Stuck in the basement
Swallowed
Ignored
Locked outside

But now
They've been welcomed home
And I am all of me
And I am here*

---

* *I AM: Poems for Expansion and Renewal*

It is good

I have made my home inside
A place of rest
That is welcoming and abundant
Full of compassion
And curiosity
A spark of life
Connected and courageous
Creativity and laughter and dance

I looked inside my home
Inside my life
(And outside too)
And I say
It is good*

---

* *I AM: Poems for Expansion and Renewal*

I am held

Now I know I am held.
Held and supported, without exception.
Without expectations. Without strings attached.

Held by Mother Earth.
Love is actually a hard word to use, even though I know
that to be true as well.
Love holds a fragrance of expectation to me.
The anticipation of love being returned.
Of constant connection.
Love and devotion.

To distinguish, I call love from Mother Earth
something else.
Supported,
Known,
Never alone.

…Never smothering,
Never expecting,
Yet never a doormat.

Always wild and free
Vibrating and flowing to its own rhythm.
Never tame or tamed…
Calling me
to the same.
The wildness, beauty, and freshness.
Her unbroken life force,
the beating heart of the world.

Mother Earth is from below, a part of me,
Always supporting me.
Immanence.*

---

* *I AM: Poems for Expansion and Renewal*

Goddess

After I have enough safety and courage and rest
in my wholeness,
I have space to explore, and connect again with the
Divine.
I find I am connected with I AM in my wholeness, but I
had no name for this mystery.
As time went on, a name emerged for the transcendent
divine:
Goddess.

She is the Moon and the Planets,
the Gravity and pull of the Tides,
She whispers the Hum,
the Vibration,
the Flow
of Life—
in and around me.
I whisper back with my Breath—
the tide of life flowing into me
and through me
and out of me.
The Breath that is me—and more than me—at the same
time.

She asks nothing of me.
I am free in her presence.

The Wisdom of Life
is simultaneously as close
and as far away as I need her to be.

Never imposing.

Always bestowing—
Self-sovereignty.

She lives in mystery
and illumination.
Cloaked in the wind…
and yet perfectly clear.

Goddess and Mother Earth dance together.
Shimmering Moonlight
A Frolicking Stream
Lush Honeysuckle
A Sigh of Contentment

I rest with them and receive these gifts
delivered on a breeze
lighting the way.*

---

* *I AM: Poems for Expansion and Renewal*

136

Chosen to Belong

"belonging to earth"—-
that phrase sits suspended
in
my
   soul;
something to
  walk
    around…
in
contemplative
             wonder.
the slow intake of possibility
  filling
      my imagination,
           my lungs,
               my heart,
                  my appetite,
     riding on expansive breath,
      then traveling down

to my soles,
resting on this earth.

I have contemplated
reciprocity,
connection,
listening,
relationship
with the earth…

I have contemplated names—
  Earth
    The Earth
      Mother Earth
Gaia
    Goddess
Immanence
    Life-giver
      Life-holder
        Life-sustainer
          Life-creator
Creator
    Co-creator
        Creatrix
all names that
          name relationship with the earth.

But belonging—
that catches my breath.
That I could be chosen
                to belong—
it feels like too much to hope for,
too much to ask,
and yet I know
          this wonder
to be true.

The Return to Myself

Simple quiet of a moment.
An inhale and exhale
The return to myself
To my body
To my moment.

Silver Strands

I have silver strands in my hair now. They glimmer in
the light. Shining back as if to say hello.
They speak of wisdom, and experience. Soul-life spoken
through threaded light on my head.
I welcome and honor them as they honor me.

I have silver strands in my hair now.
They glimmer in the light.
Shining back as if to say hello.

They speak of wisdom,
and experience.
Soul-life
spoken
through threaded light
on my head.
I welcome
and honor them
as they honor me.

I no longer have rules posted inside

I no longer have rules posted inside
…or anyone enforcing them.

Instead I have a table—
A round table,
An abundant table,

Where we all gather
and laugh
and share stories.

We work together,
share heartaches,
and struggles together.

We share when we annoy each other
when we're frustrated and
want something different.

We listen—
we figure out what that different is
together
so we can all be here—together.

No one left out,
no one in the shadows,
no one in the basement,
no one in the attic,

No one watching, or evaluating, or judging—

No one we have to please,
or live up to.
We're just here
...and it's Amazing.*

* *I AM: Poems for Expansion and Renewal*

Trust is like a contented cat

I love this trusting thing.
Where I trust you to know what's best for you,
And I trust me to know what's best for me.

I feel like a contented cat,
curled up and purring.
Stretching and going to play,
enjoying my food,
licking my paws,
and lying down again,
purring and at peace.

I have a tree of wisdom and life

I have a tree of wisdom and life
inside me

Lush and abundant
Majestic and bold

It grows out of nothing

I clear the ground
of shrapnel
left from the days
of unknowing—

The ground becomes a desert.

Then a Goddess appears.

I do not know her name,
Only that she comes from the ground—
the ground of my life
at the core of my soul;
she sits with patience
and daring:
An invitation to live and be at rest.

As my parts gather and play,
climbing on her weighty breasts
they knew they are home and it is safe.

I do not have to ask for anything,

I do not have to struggle.

The Tree comes next—
in an instant it grows:

Antonio's magic Encanto Tree
comes to life
in my core:

I sit with my back against its trunk;
I receive its support,
I receive its love,
…and its knowing.

I know
Divine Wisdom is inside me.
She is with me,
She watches over me,
She is me,
I am home.*

---

* *I AM: Poems for Expansion and Renewal*

What happens on the inside

The gift of
seeing
knowing
sensing
my inner world.

Met and unmet needs
in the form of
emotions
sensations
hunger
pain
fear
exhaustion
speak to me.

I am continually aware
of these cues
and clues
from my body.
Some are loud
        and insistent.
                They distract me
    and cause discomfort
                until I answer their call.

Some call softly,
whisper-quiet.
I check in regularly
to make sure I don't miss them.

Life Raft Emotions

Emotions—

They carry me through
the hardest times
as if they were
a sherpa,
a piggy-backing parent,
a hammock,
a steamboat,
a life raft,
a trampoline,
a zip line…
they see me through.

They guide me through
the murkiest times
as if they were
a flashlight,
twinkle lights,
a beacon,
a headlamp,
a candle
a full moon's glow…
they light a path forward.

They speak to me through
the most confusing times
as if they were
a wise seer,
a guru's apprentice,

a hope-enfuser,
a quote-creator,
a safe haven,
a loyal friend…
they communicate clarity.

I know the way

I know the way
In some ways, the way is
Inside
And also outside

It's more like a compass

I have a compass at my core
Pointing me
in My direction

Holding me near
Centering me
Bringing the sifted past
To point the way forward

And sending me forth like a bird in flight
Holding me up from below

As I soar overhead
I know the way
The way is inside me
And reaches before me*

I AM: Poems for Expansion and Renewal

My feelings nourish me

I am in awe of my heart
How can it hold so many feelings
So many
At the same time
They jostle for attention
For space
They sit down politely
(sometimes)

They give my life fullness
Vitality
The spark of life
Fireworks exploding into the sky
In excitement
A quiet ebb of grief
Sometimes a rumble of thunder or earthquake of anger
But they're all there
Navigating me through this life
Helping me know what I need
Who I am

My feelings nourish me
And I release them to do their work*

---

* *I AM: Poems for Expansion and Renewal*

Held and Free

I can see myself at the edge of a tall plateau.
I can feel the achingly beautiful warm air cooling and
lightly swirling...
In almost a pause, but not quite
The enjoyment of every moment,
each moment
a delicious
pause—
stretching out—----
longing for it to go further.
I can feel its sweet ache of satisfaction stretching out like
taffy across the precipice,
a sigh so deep...pregnant with longing and full of my
life and sustenance

And I feel held and free
(thank you, Glennon Doyle, for that phrase)

I am all things and everything
caressed and mysterious
known and anticipated
the hammock breath of quiet

held
free
melding yet separate
atoms intertwining in a caress
and delightfully bouncing off as on a trampoline
jumping for joy
to be in

and new
and old
and the same
and once again
and all things
once more.

A new cosmology is birthed in me
and around me and in me
and all through me.
Not taking over
Not asking or coercing.
How do I describe the invitation that is at once inviting
and also completely free of any pressure or need from
me?
Alluring but not tempting
Inviting but not needy
Clear but not blinding
A welcome with both longing for me to enter and
complete trust in me to be wholly where I am to be.
Trust in time, in the universe, in the order of things, to be
right, to be where they are, to be full and free.
Appreciation
Seen— but not in a spotlight
Known— but not pinned down
Understood— but not labeled
Welcome— but not smothered

The holy essence of being.
The intergalactic and microscopic
and cosmic and quiet
The mundane and the glorious

The magical light spores dancing with dust
We are now
We are eternal
We are dust
We are forever
We are for this moment
We are

It's Ironic

it's ironic
and amazing
that coming home to yourself,
trusting yourself,
isn't an act of rugged individualism.
it's a level of autonomy
that allows you to live
fully and completely
inside of yourself
and
naturally connect to all of life—
you are not isolated,
but actually more connected
by connecting to yourself,
you are reconnecting with the
mycelium of life

Intuition

The world of the third eye
and prophecy
and unveiling
are becoming a part of my daily being.
Like wispy haze solidifying into transparent, luminous
shapes and forms.
It feels like I am in another world, and yet right here, in
the world I have always been.
I am more real.
I am more solid.
And so is this connection and awareness.
Intuition is not a gift I have,
something that makes me special.
It is my eyes, my ears, my taste, my touch, my
connection. It is a sense.
It is not something that makes me more enlightened. It is
a part of my humanity.
It is more like getting glasses so you can see more
sharply.
Slowing down so you can feel the warmth of the sun on
your skin.
Being ready.
And awake.*

---

* *Awakening Wonder*

Self-Trust

A gift we are born with,
One who supports and surrounds us
with Her loving arms.

Inner Wisdom,
an inner compass
filled with wonder.

When I Trust Myself

My soul is singing
humming
vibrating
with excitement
or contentment.
there is subtle, rhythmic movement
confidence
surety
fullness
conviction
rightness
aliveness
inspiration
seeing across time and space
a moment submerged in soul-space
touching more than my soul
my space
my moment in time
connected together
in stillness
reflection
release
celebration.

My chest swells
my heart feels full,
large, expansive,
luminous love
warming all I'm connected to
in its soft warm glow.

My gut is wise and knowing.
It feels steady,
sure,
supple and strong.

My chest and diaphragm expand
full, deep, breaths.
The breaths in
feel soul-nourishing.
The exhales complete,
lacking nothing in their release.

Everything feels
like
clean
clear
smooth
water
or air
or fog
or breath
or being.

It all flows together.
All together.
And all their own sovereigns.

My feet feel sure on the ground.
My legs feel ready
for movement,
no longer stuck

and weighed down
by tight muscles.

I feel both alert and calm.
Inspired
Energized
Ready.

My mind is
clear
knowing
bowing to the wisdom
from within
and without.
It affirms,
"yes."
We know.
Yes.
We agree.
Yes.
We love you.
Yes.
We are wise.
My third eye sees
past the horizon
across space and time
to all soul-connection.
An eon encountered in a moment.

We are more

We are muscles and fascia
We are bones
We are blood
We are organs
We are epidermis and hormones and neurotransmitters
We are all these
and more.

We are complex emotion
and psyche
and soul
motivation
intention
action
desire.

body mechanics
the ability to move
and feel what is inside and outside
we are all these
and more.

We are families and communities and individuals and
countries and continents and tribes and cultures.
We are colors and heights and voice tones and...
Personalities and actions and reactions
And politics and sociology
Animals and humans
We are more.

She accepts

I have found myself at the entrance
to the cave.

The red thread is still in my hand,
the story of where I've traveled,
and what I've shed.
So many layers no longer needed,
gifted to the stone floor.

I face outward
away from the cave
anticipation coursing through my veins.

I am alive.
I am fierce.
I am tender.
I am here.

I feel ready
for the wrapping up of my senses
with all earth's glory:

A breathful of pine scent travels through
my being
with crisp
aliveness.

The wind
blowing against
 my body—

a proprioceptive experience long
 longed for.

The air filled with water
blurring my vision.
And encompassing me at
the same time.
Like a gentle arm across
my shoulders.

We are here.
We have been waiting
for you.
Your magic is potent.
It calls out to our alchemizing abilities
to come forth.

The trees sway their welcome,
and an offer of mentorship.

A tree nymph,
a fierce goddess,
a divine being connected,
anchored in this time and space,
steps forth
and
She
accepts.

164

About the Author

Catherine Quiring, MA, LMHC is a Licensed Mental Health Counselor, and Self-Trust Coach. She helps people who feel and care deeply to reconnect to their inner wisdom, heal from the pressures and traumas they have experienced, reclaim their playfulness, and liberate through collective care.

Catherine hosts the podcast Who We Are & What We Need, and is the author of *I AM: Poems for Expansion and Renewal, Awakening Wonder: Embracing Kinship with all of Life,* and *Neurodiverse Musings: Reflections on my Neurodivergent Existence.*

Catherine is a cis-gendered, female, white, thin, neuroqueer, intuitive empath. She is a reformed people-pleaser and decolonizing exvangelical. She is an advocate for intersectional anti-oppressive work. Catherine names what she knows of herself at this time in her journey to let you know that whatever your personal identifications, you are welcome here.

Outside of work, Catherine is an avid book-lover, paddleboard enthusiast, parent to two amazing kids who invite her into the adventure of every-day life, and partner to a very tall husband who makes her laugh and helps her rest.

Connect with Catherine at www.catherinequiring.com.

Made in United States
Orlando, FL
05 July 2025

62668191R00105